On Their Own

Adventure Athletes in Solo Sports

By Steve Boga

BOOK THREE

HNB

HIGH NOON BOOKS
Novato, California

International Standard Book Number: 0-87879-927-3

0 9 8 7 6 5
0 9 8 7 6 5 4 3

Library of Congress Cataloging-in-Publication Data

Boga, Steve. 1947—
    On their own: adventure athletes in solo sports/ by Steve Boga.
        p.   cm.
    Summary: Describes the training, determination, and personal triumphs of such athletes as motorcycle racer Kenny Roberts, long distance runner Ann Trason, and speed skater Eric Heiden.
    ISBN 0-87879-928-1
    1. Athletes—United States—Biography.   2. Determination (Personality trait) [1. Athletes.] I. Title.
GV697.A1B555   1992
796'.092'2—dc20
[B]   92-15762
                                         CIP
                                         AC

Contents

Greg LeMond—Fame and Fortune on a Bike

Greg LeMond
Wheels of Fortune

Greg LeMond is the most famous bicycle racer in the world. He is also the richest bicycle racer. He makes more than $4 million a year from his bike. Yet when Greg was a kid, bicycling was not even one of his favorite sports.

When Greg was 7 years old, his family moved to beautiful Lake Tahoe in California. He says, "Moving to the mountains really opened my eyes to the outdoors. I fell in love with sports like backpacking, hunting, fishing, and skiing."

He really loved skiing. His dad also skied. The two of them would drive all around the mountains. They looked for the best slopes. Then they skied all day.

But Greg soon got tired of riding a ski lift up a hill and skiing right back down. He wanted more of a challenge. He wanted a greater thrill. He says, "I liked free style skiing. I wanted to be an acrobat on skis. I wanted to do the aerial flips I had seen on TV."

That kind of skiing is called "hot dog" skiing. Greg asked his parents if he could go to a training camp for hot dog skiers. While he was there, he hurt his back and could not do flips. But he still learned a lot at the camp. The teachers told him to bicycle. They said it was the best workout if he wanted to ski.

He thought about it. He and his dad had just watched a big-time bike race go right by their house. Greg was thrilled by the speed, the action, and the effort. "Those guys have to be so fit," he thought.

So Greg started riding a bike. He says, "At

first, cycling seemed like hard work to me. But I wanted to be a great skier. If cycling would help me ski better, I thought a little hard work couldn't hurt."

Greg's father again joined his son in his new sport. Dad decided biking was a good way to lose 20 pounds. He and Greg began riding bikes about 20 miles a day. Soon they were climbing mountain passes on their bikes. "I was lucky that my dad loved the sport so much," Greg admits.

Greg loved the sport, too. For the next few years, he did nothing else but ride his bike. "I was so hooked on my bike that I did not hunt, fish or ski anymore," Greg says.

He and his dad entered races. Greg started winning right away. He won 30 races in his first year. Nobody in his age group could keep up with him. So he started racing older kids.

When he was 15, he entered the Tour of Fresno. It was a "stage race." That meant the riders raced more than one day. The Tour of Fresno was a three-day race. You had to race hard, then come back the next day and do it again.

Also in the race was John Howard. John was the best road racer in the United States. Greg was just a skinny kid. But the skinny kid finished second. He was only 10 seconds behind John after three days of racing. He says, "That race turned a lot of heads. I was a high school sophomore, not yet shaving, and I almost beat John Howard."

At age 16, Greg became Junior National Champion. At age 18, he became Junior World Champion. The next year he got married. Then he signed a contract with a pro team in France. That was a big deal. If Greg wanted to ride in the "big leagues," he had to go to Europe. And only one American had ever been good enough to race for a European pro team.

So Greg and his wife Kathy flew off to

France. They were only 19 years old. It was hard at first for them in France. They were away from home. They did not know anybody. They did not speak French. The owner of the team had promised Greg $100,000, a car, and a house. But the car did not work. The house was cold and had no furniture. And the money was always late. They were unhappy.

Greg went on road trips just like a baseball player. He was the only one on the team who did not speak French. That made him feel lonely. He read a lot of books. Back at the house Kathy also felt lonely. They almost quit and went back to America. Greg says, "We came from nice families. But in France we had no friends, no heat, no furniture, no money— nothing! We did not speak French. There were no American movies. There was not even a McDonald's restaurant."

On top of that, Greg's racing was not going well. Says Greg, "It rained every day. I trained about 60 miles a day, and it rained, rained, rained. I could not get in shape."

Greg did not do well in his first few races. He says, "Right from the start, I was at the back. I just could not believe how fast they were going. I was in shock."

He was so depressed. Sometimes when people feel that bad, they give up. They quit. Others, like Greg, fight back. They work through the bad feelings.

After one bad finish in a long race, Greg went riding for an hour. It was dark when he finally returned. The next week, after another bad finish, he went riding for two hours. The worse he raced, the harder he worked. He rode when he was sick. He rode when it was freezing outside. "I didn't want to ride all the time, but I was dedicated," he says."

He sure was dedicated. And talented. Put the two together and the result is often success. When Greg was 20, he returned to the United

States for a race. It was called the Coors Classic. It was thrilling to come "home." Then he won the race! The man Greg beat was from the Soviet Union. He was the gold-medal winner in the 1980 Olympics. Greg had wanted that gold medal. But the U.S. had not gone to that Olympics.

Then in 1986, he won the Tour de France. The Tour is a huge stage race. It takes more than three weeks. It goes all around France. Every day the best riders in the world race 60 to 100 miles. They total up the riders' time. The low time wins.

Thousands of people line the roads to watch and cheer the riders. It is the most famous bike race in the world. It is like the World Series in baseball. No American had ever won the Tour de France before Greg. He was now the best in the world.

Then he had a terrible accident.

Greg had grown up around guns. He took hunters' safety courses. He entered contests. He felt safe around guns.

As an adult, he did not hunt during the bicycle season. But in April of 1987, Greg was home with a broken bone in his hand. The day before he was due to go back to Europe, he went hunting with his uncle. His brother-in-law, Pat, also came along. Pat had never hunted before.

The three men hiked up a hill. They were looking for wild turkeys. Finally they decided to split up. Uncle Rod went left and brother Pat went right. Greg stayed put. After awhile Greg heard Pat whistle. He was trying to find out where Greg was. But Greg decided to stay quiet. After all, if he could tell it was a human whistle, so could the turkeys.

Greg knew how he would tell Pat where he was. He would stand up. He reached a crouch. A shot rang out! It was so loud that Greg thought his own gun had gone off. He fell back to earth like a rock. For a second, he did not know that he had been hit. Then he saw blood on his hand. Then his whole body went numb.

He tried to stand, but he almost passed out. He tried to call out, but he could not breathe. His right lung had collapsed. And his body was in shock.

When Pat found out that he had shot the best known bicycle racer in the world, he fell apart. So Greg's uncle had to run home and call 911.

Then Greg got lucky. There was a rescue helicopter nearby. The pilot heard the call for help and went to Greg. He got Greg to the hospital in 10 minutes. That saved his life. The doctor said that he would not have lived through a long ambulance ride.

Greg had 60 buck shot pellets in his body. They were in his liver, his kidneys, and his heart lining. Doctors pulled out half of them.

They left the other half in. They said his body would heal on its own. They were right.

But the pain was intense. Says Greg, "I never thought I would be the type to need pain killers. I thought I was used to pain on my bike. But that is not pain. What you feel on your bike is nothing compared to real pain. I think of that sometimes when I ride."

For a long time, it looked as if Greg would never ride again. He came home but could do nothing. He says, "The pain lasted for 3 or 4 weeks. I would sit in a chair at home shaking with pain. Sweat would run down my face. I would cry and cry. It hurt so much."

He lost 15 pounds in the first 2 weeks. He could only shuffle from bed to chair. After 3 weeks he could walk 2 blocks. Five weeks after he was shot, he went fishing. But he was tired after 20 minutes.

Then he started riding his bike. He was very slow. But it felt good just to be back on his bike. Then Greg started riding with another man. The man was not a pro racer. He was just a guy with a bike. And he was a little fat. But he could beat Greg. "Here I had won the Tour de France, and now I was being left behind by some guy riding the back roads of California!"

Then one day Greg beat that guy. He was firmly on the road back to the top.

If Greg had died that day, it would have changed bicycling history. The slender young man still had great things to do. He brought himself all the way back to the top. He won the Tour de France in 1989. After 23 days and more than 90 hours of riding, Greg won by 8 seconds. Some called it the most exciting bike race ever. And some people think it is the greatest comeback in the history of sports.

Then Greg won the Tour de France again in 1990. It was his third win in that race. Only 5 riders have ever won 3 Tours de France.

And Greg is not done yet.

Shirley Metz Ready for a Day in Antartica

Shirley Metz
South Pole Skier

Shirley was born in Minnesota on May 3, 1949. "It is a cold state," she says. "It's about the only thing in my past that gives a clue to my going to the South Pole."

There were, in fact, other clues. Her father was in the Air Force, so she learned to travel. "I was born in the United States, but I went to school all over the world," she says.

Shirley also learned as a kid how to be alone. She says, "I found out I better not make friends. I knew if I got close to someone, I would lose them when we moved."

She was a shy, quiet little girl. That was just the way her mother liked it. She thought children should be seen and not heard. Shirley says, "My mother was one of those people who always thought she was right. But I loved her just the same. She broke a few wooden spoons on me. But she also taught me that if you're going to do a job, you do it right. Not just to the best of your ability, but until it's done."

She went to high school in Hawaii. She was a good athlete. Surfing and scuba diving were her best sports.

Her family moved away from Hawaii. Shirley stayed behind to go to college. Her parents thought that was fine. But they gave her no money. She had to work three part-time jobs to pay for school.

The summer after college, she met Dick Metz. He was a lot older than Shirley. But he was fit and looked young. He was also rich. He was a partner with a man named Hobie. They had a chain that was called Hobie Sports Shops. They sold clothes and gear for skiing, surfing, and sailing.

Dick taught Shirley how to ski and sail. Then he married her.

Shirley and Dick moved to Southern California. They managed one sports shop and started many others. They started 15 stores in 15 years. Then they sold out. That made Shirley rich, too.

Some people think that money solves all your problems. But it can make brand-new problems. Shirley suddenly had more money than she ever dreamed she would have. But she was not happy. She didn't know what she was going to do with her life. That was important to her. She was not yet 40 years old. She had lots of life yet. She had to do something with the rest of her years. But what?

At the last minute, she decided to go on vacation with Dick's mother. She would think about her future while she was gone. They took a 3-week cruise to Antarctica. "I had always wanted to see the penguins," Shirley says.

They sailed from a town in Chile called Puntas Arenas. It is the world's most southern city. The ship took them even farther south. Soon there were icebergs all around them. They glistened in the sun. Some looked like table tops. Others looked like huge diamonds. All of them looked fantastic.

Like most Americans, Shirley didn't know much about Antarctica. She only knew that it was cold, icy, and way down south. She says, "On the globes in school, they put it on the bottom and stick a screw through it. None of us ever really looks at it."

Shirley saw at once that there was no place like it on earth. It was wild. It was peaceful. It was beautiful. She fell in love with it.

Back home she wanted to know more about the "frozen continent." She went to lectures and meetings. She learned, for example, that Antarctica has 90% of the world's fresh water.

It's all in the form of ice. But Antarctica is also a desert. Away from the coast, it only rains and snows 2 inches a year.

She also learned that Antarctica needed protection. A treaty had been signed in 1961 by many nations. It was supposed to protect Antarctica. But it was only good until 1991. And what then? Some countries have talked of drilling for oil there. "If that happened," Shirley thought, "Antarctica would be ruined."

Shirley met Martyn Williams. He was an outdoor guide who had been to Antarctica. Shirley was impressed with Martyn. He shared her love for Antarctica. She loved to listen to him talk about that wild place.

Martyn was also impressed with Shirley. He thought she had a certain inner strength. He told her, "I'm planning a ski trip to the South Pole. We will ski about 750 miles. Why don't you come along?"

She laughed. "Don't be silly. I do intend to

go back to Antarctica. But I don't plan to ski to the South Pole," she said.

But the idea stayed with her. She couldn't stop thinking about it. She says, "I saw my life as 3 parts. In the first 20 years, there was school. In the next 20 years, there was work, a career. In the 3rd part, I was supposed to do the things I had learned about in the first 2 parts."

She had become a good skier. She was strong. She was willing to work hard. And she wanted to do something different. She thought, "Maybe I can ski to the South Pole. Maybe I should do it. It would be a thrill. Plus, it would be a good way to spread the word about Antarctica."

She called Martyn back and said she would ski to the South Pole. When her husband heard about it, he nearly went into shock.

———————

Two months later, Shirley, Martyn and 9

other people were skiing across Antarctica. They moved in a straight line. They were heading right for the South Pole. Their compass told them so.

They needed that compass. They had to keep their heads down. A strong head wind blasted them. Snow flew all around them. The sky was the same color as the ground—white!

Shirley could not tell if the snow was falling from the sky or blowing up from the ground. Her whole world was white. And all she could hear was the howl of the wind. She started talking to herself. "I wanted to do this . . . I chose to do this," she kept saying over and over.

That night in her tent, Shirley wrote this in her diary:

We started this trip on the edge of the Ronne Ice Shelf close to sea level. The South Pole is 9,300 feet above sea level. So we are always climbing.

As we go south, the air gets colder and the

ice gets harder. It's so slick at times that we slide around like cats on a marble floor. We have to make it to the South Pole before February 1st. It will be too cold after that.

We ski 13, 14, sometimes 15 miles each day. The wind is always in our faces. It can break your heart. We try to pace ourselves and keep moving. That's better than stopping a lot. If you stop for very long here, you will freeze to death.

We take turns being in front. Leading is very hard. We change leaders every hour. When you lead, you have to pick a point on the horizon and head right for it. It's usually nothing more than a shadow. There are no trees. The leader gets hit with more wind than anyone else. That means you fall down a lot. I call it "Hero Hour."

At night (which is as light as day), we stop to make camp. We put up our huge tent. That's the dining and meeting room. Then we put up our two-man tents. Finally, we dig the ice latrines. When the stoves get going in the big tent, it gets up to about freezing (32 degrees F.) in there. It's the warmest place for hundreds of miles.

24

I will be the first one up in the morning. I always am. It's the best time for me to get things done. I use that time to write my poetry and to think. I learned long ago how to get things done. You just sleep less.

Two weeks later Shirley again wrote in her diary:

It's funny—I live close to 10 other people. But this is really a lonely trip. In the days, we wear masks to protect us from the howling wind. So we rarely talk. For most of the 9 hours that we ski, we are locked in our own thoughts.

I truly like all the people. But there are some I would do this trip with again. And there are some I would not. I guess that makes sense.

At first our group stopped any time someone needed to stop. But that did not work very well. Someone always needed to stop. So now we stop 5 minutes every hour.

That keeps us together. We have learned there is no point in getting way ahead. You will freeze to death waiting for the others to catch up.

There are so many things to do during those 5 minutes. As we get near the breaks, I figure out what I am going to do first. Do I want to change the film in the camera? Should I eat? If it's a potty stop, I may spend the whole 5 minutes just trying to get dressed again.

Later, she wrote this:

At first I was always lagging behind. The others must have wondered if I would keep up. But now I am getting stronger. Some of the others are getting weaker. I think it is because I was in shape when we left. Some of the men have lost a lot of weight, but I have stayed about the same. I bet Joe loses 30 pounds.

There are no showers out here. But I cannot go 2 months without bathing. So I have found a way. I pour my leftover drinking water into the lid of my thermos. Then I take a Handiwipe bath.

We eat really well here. Nothing spoils. Antarctica is a huge ice box. We even have fresh eggs. They were broken into plastic bags before we left. We also have bacon, sausage, peanut butter, granola, and bread. For dinner, it's shrimp or beef. We have to have dishes rich in fat. In this cold, our bodies crave fat. I eat a cube of butter a day. I munch on it like a candy bar.

We recycle everything except toilet paper. That gets buried. No food gets thrown out. If you don't finish your oatmeal, you will find it in your dinner.

When I get home, people will ask, "How did you deal with the cold?" My answer will be, "Not bad." Mostly I think it's mind over matter. I say to myself, "O.K., I am cold, but I have to accept it. I have to work through it. I'm cold, keep going. I'm tired, keep going."

So that we won't freeze in our sleeping bag, we have to warm up before we get in. Martyn's advice is always the same. "Shovel snow!" he says. I've decided that we never really get warm. We only get less cold.

Worse than the cold are the blisters on my feet. I have blisters on my blisters. I have taped pieces of my sleeping pad around my poor feet. Everyone has blisters, but none worse than mine. We have all changed to larger boots to try to relieve the pain. I'm *lucky. I have the smallest feet, so I can wear anyone's boots.*

Near the end of the trip, Shirley again wrote in her diary:

Some of the others have started to count down the days. I hear them say, "Only six days left . . . only five days left . . . four . . . three . . ." Why do they want it to be over? Don't they know that they will never be here again? I try to take each day at a time. And I find myself moving away from those guys who are counting the days.

For days the group had been worried that they would miss the Pole. But then they saw it! It was only a black speck. "There's the American base," someone cried. And they knew they were right on target. "Three cheers!" someone else yelled. And they all felt great.

They no longer needed a compass. They walked the last few miles side by side. They held their heads up. They were proud. They had all done it! No one had died. No one had quit.

The 60 workers at the base greeted them. They shook hands and slapped the skiers on the back. Shirley thought something more was needed. So she went around and hugged everyone.

Later Shirley posed for pictures. For a laugh, she posed in her underwear. Behind her in the picture, a sign reads:

GEOGRAPHIC SOUTH POLE
9,301 FOOT ELEVATION
AVERAGE TEMPERATURE –55 DEGREES

Now Shirley gives talks about her trip. She travels and tells people how we must save Antarctica. Just as she thought, people always ask her about the cold.

Yes, she admits, it was cold at the South Pole in her underwear. Then she laughs. "But I warmed up by running around the world in about two minutes. It's not every day you get to run around the world in your underwear."

Peter Hackett and a Sherpa Friend

Peter Hackett
Mountain Doctor

Peter Hackett was not much of an athlete as a kid. The captains of the gym teams picked him last for baseball. Then they put him out in right field. They made him an end in football. But they never threw the ball to him.

Peter was the oldest of 10 brothers. His father was a doctor. Dad traveled a lot. So Peter often played daddy to the younger kids. He says, "So much is expected of the oldest child. I was often the one in charge. Maybe being head of the house made me achieve."

When he was a teenager, Peter watched his best friend die. The friend had hit his head on the side of a swimming pool. Peter sat nearby while doctors tried to save his life. He felt helpless. He recalls thinking, "I wish I knew enough to help."

He decided it would not happen again. After college, he went to medical school. Like his dad, he would be a doctor.

After school, Peter went to work at San Francisco General Hospital. He was supposed to go back to Chicago after a year. He was supposed to become a partner in his dad's medical practice. But Peter soon knew that he did not want to work in the city. He says, "I saw almost every stab and gun shot victim in the city. I got sick of all the violence."

He left the city and went to the mountains. He bought boots and a back pack. He bought dried food. He went hiking in Yosemite for 2 weeks. When he came off the trail, he knew for sure he could not go back to the city. So he asked around in Yosemite for a job. He was hired to help save climbers who had fallen.

He lived in a tent cabin. His best friend was the owl that lived next door. When he was not working, he learned how to climb. Says Peter, "The whole summer was great. I loved the outdoors. And I loved climbing. It is a sport that gives you quick results. Either you make the move or you don't make the move. To do it right you have to focus on the move. You cannot do a move if you are thinking about something else."

Peter became a good climber. He was not a big guy. He looked skinny. But he was strong for his size. And he knew his way around rock. He felt at home in the mountains.

He looked for work that would let him stay in the mountains—any mountains!

His next job was in Nepal. It is a country near India. Nepal has the highest mountains in the world. They make the ones in the United States look like ant hills.

Peter wanted to see Mt. Everest, the highest

mountain in the world. (It is 29,028 feet above sea level.) So he signed on with a travel group. They needed a doctor to hike with them all summer. Peter took care of the hikers who were sick or hurt.

It was in Nepal that Peter first learned about "mountain sickness." On his first hike to the Everest Base Camp about half of his group got sick. They were about 18,000 feet above sea level. Many people had what seemed like the flu. Their heads ached and they were throwing up. Peter later found out that they had mountain sickness.

He wanted to know more about it. He wanted to study why people got sick in the mountains. So he chose to live in the high mountains. He lived with a tribe called the Sherpas. Peter spent a winter living in a little hut. It had a dirt floor. It also had stone walls with lots of holes in them. Dirt and cold air blew right through the hut.

Peter took care of the Sherpas in the village. He learned their language. He even adopted two children. In return the people brought him food or clothes. Says Peter, "I would put up a sign. It would say, 'The doctor needs a new pair of pants' or 'The doctor needs potatoes.' And they would bring them."

Peter heard that a team of American doctors planned to try to climb Mt. Everest. He wanted to be a part of that team. He could keep doing his research on mountain sickness. Plus he might get to climb the tallest mountain in the world.

Peter applied for the trip. He was accepted. He had made the team. He was going to climb Mt. Everest!

———————

Several months later, Peter lay in his sleeping bag on Mt. Everest. He felt dull and tired. He was 26,000 feet above sea level. The air was cold and very thin. There was not as much

35

oxygen as at sea level. That made it hard to breathe. And they had so much work to do.

It was 2 A.M. and still dark. But it was time to get up. If they wanted to get to the top of Mt. Everest, they had to start early. "When you are 5 miles above sea level, it takes a long time to do anything," Peter thought.

Peter woke up his partner, Chris Pizzo. Then he went to the other tent and woke up the two Sherpas. Then he began to melt ice on his tiny stove. That was where they got their drinking water. They had to drink lots of water. "The body dries out fast up here," Peter thought.

Two hours later the four men were moving up the mountain. It was still dark. Chris was tied to one Sherpa, and Peter was tied to the other one. They used ice axes to help them up and over the snow.

Chris's team went ahead. The Sherpa with Peter got cold. His feet began to freeze. He went back. Now Peter was climbing alone. Two hours later he passed Chris and the Sherpa. They had made it to the top and were on their way back down.

"I don't know whether I should keep going," said Peter.

"Are you climbing well?" Chris asked.

"Yes," said Peter.

"Well then, go for it! The weather is good. And you may never be this close to the top of Mt. Everest again," said Chris.

That was all Peter needed. Chris's words pushed him on. He said goodbye to Chris, then moved up the mountain.

He later stopped to rest on the edge of a sheer drop. "I am near the top of the world," he thought. He was breathing hard through his air mask. He was always breathing hard. Even taking one step was hard work.

A cold wind hit him hard. It blew snow into his face. It was not the first time in his life that snow had hit him in the face. But this time was different. This time he was alone at 28,000 feet above sea level. It was real scary!

He thought about quitting. "I could sit right here for a while. Then I could go back down and say that I made it to the top. No, I could never do that. It would not be right. Plus I would freeze to death if I stayed here."

He came to a ridge. There was only one way to go. He dug his axe into the ice. Then he pulled himself up on the ridge. He flopped onto a rock like a beached whale. It took 2 minutes for his heart to slow down.

Suddenly he saw a dead body! It was a woman. She was frozen in the ice. The cold had preserved the body. She looked like she had died yesterday. She still had her clothes and boots on. Peter remembers thinking, "I've seen a lot of dead bodies. But this is the first time I have ever had to climb over one."

He looked up. In front of him was a 900-

foot wall of ice. It was straight up, a tall fang that seemed to cut into the sky. "How am I going to climb that?" he wondered.

He looked down. Clouds blocked his view. He thought, "If I fall, I will roll all the way to sea level." The rest of his team was somewhere below, but he could not see them. And all he could hear was the wind and the sound of his own breathing.

"I am committed to try for the top. Either I make it to the top or I die," he said to himself.

He inched his way up the steep ridge of ice. He would take 2 steps. Then he would stop and breathe 20 times. Any fall here would kill him. Even a broken ankle at this height would kill him. There was nobody to help him.

Three times he thought he was at the top. But it was only a trick that the mountain was playing on him. Then he saw that it was down on all sides. He had made it! He was on top of the world!

The top was a tiny flat spot. It was scary standing on that windy piece of snow. But Peter had to do it. He had come a long way. It had taken months to get here. He had lost 15 pounds. He had a bad cough. He had frostnip on his toes. But at that moment he was the highest person on earth!

He could see forever. It was thrilling! But it was getting late. The wind had picked up. Peter decided, "There are no hotels up here. I better start back."

He took some pictures to prove that he had made it to the top. Then he started back home. "It took me months to get here. And then I spend only 15 minutes at the top," he thought.

He gave a silent thanks to the mountain for letting him get to the top. Then he asked that it let him get back down.

It was not easy. Going down can be harder than going up. Many people have died trying to get down from Everest. Peter had to face the mountain. He dug his ice axe into the snow. Then he kicked steps into the ice. He moved down as if he were on a ladder.

Suddenly he broke loose. He was falling! It seemed as if it were all in slow motion. He had time to think, "This cannot be happening. I am not ready to die. But that is what I am going to do. And it is so easy . . . "

Then all of a sudden, he was not falling anymore. "Holy cow! I'm not dead," he realized.

Peter was hanging upside down by his knees. His legs were wedged behind a rock. If he had missed that rock, he would have fallen about 7,000 feet. They never would have found his body.

He was all right. He again thanked the mountain. Then he thought how much he loved life. He thought how much he wanted to live. "And that is just what I am going to do," he thought.

Jan Case in Full Flight

Jan Case
Winged Wonder

Jan Case likes to say that love of flying is "in her blood." Her father was a Navy pilot. He took Jan to lots of air shows. She watched other pilots do stunts. It thrilled her. Little Jan wondered what it would be like to fly like a bird.

She grew up a tomboy. "My mother let me be what I wanted to be," she says. And what she wanted to be was an athlete. "When I was 4, I was skiing with Dad and my 2 brothers. I was water skiing by the time I was 8 years old. And I was canoeing and sailing," she says.

When she was 15, her brother brought home a Navy buddy. His name was Lee. Jan says, "Lee came for a visit and stayed a year. He was 20 and like a big brother to me."

Lee didn't want to be Jan's big brother. He was in love with her. But he was willing to wait until she was an adult. He left for a couple of years. Then he showed up at her door on the day she turned 18.

They dated for a while. Then Lee told her, "I love you. I will marry you. But first you need to grow up. Go to college. Have some fun."

She took his advice. She went off to Western Washington College. There she learned something about herself. She learned that she loved teaching but hated school. "It was 1968. There were other things to do besides go to school," she says.

So Jan quit college. She went to work as a secretary. But she didn't last long at that job. She was soon fired. She wasn't meant to work in an office.

She got a job teaching skiing. She found out that she loved to teach sports. So she also taught water safety. "I found out I loved being with people who were learning how to play. When people are learning a new sport, they are the best they can be."

After teaching all winter, she called Lee in San Francisco. "I've grown up," she told him.

"Come on home," he said.

So she went back to California to be with him.

Lee was a tough little guy. He was also an athlete. Jan says, "He was a surfer and a skier. He was one of those guys who thought he could do anything. He was usually right."

Lee also read a lot of books. One day he picked up a book about flying. It became his next passion. But he did not want to fly planes. He wanted to fly hang gliders. That was the new sport. A hang glider is like a kite. The pilot holds on to a control bar shaped like a triangle. The bar hangs below the kite. That's how the pilot steers the kite. He can feel the wind in his face like a bird.

At first Jan thought the sport was crazy. But then she, too, learned to love it. She and Lee started a business. They opened Chandelle Sky Sails (hang gliders were first called "sky sails"). They made hang gliders. Jan sewed the kites. They also taught others how to fly them. That was another of Jan's jobs. She taught flying.

"Some thought it was odd that I was teaching before I was flying. But it made sense. Teaching something is not the same as doing something. I can teach juggling even though I can't juggle three balls. I can look at things and take them apart. I can see what is going on. And then I can explain it to other people. I am a teacher," she says.

Lee became a great pilot. Jan says, "Back in the early 1970s, that meant he could steer the glider pretty much where he wanted to go and then land on his feet most of the time."

But Jan still had not flown. One reason, she claimed, was her size. She was 5 feet tall and weighed 95 pounds. The gliders back then weighed 50 pounds. If she wanted to fly off a hill, she had to carry the glider up the hill. "By the time I got to the top of a hill, I was too tired to fly," she says.

Then her friends built Jan a lighter glider. "They shamed me into flying," she says. On the one hand, she felt proud. Her friends cared about her, she thought. On the other hand, she felt fear—intense fear!

She hung her glider harness in the shop. Then she tied herself into it. She would just hang there for hours, getting used to how it felt. Then she began carrying the glider around with her. She was trying to make friends with it.

Then one day she hauled the glider to the

top of a hill. She set it up and sat next to it. It was windy. And the winds kept changing. She looked out at space. Then she looked down the hill. She saw a tree half way down. She saw herself landing in that tree. It did not seem like a good idea. So she picked up her glider and went back home.

One day Jan woke up and knew she was going to fly. She let Lee carry her glider up the hill. She wanted to be strong for her first flight.

Lee acted as if he did not care if Jan flew. He told her she was the one who had to decide. "He was giving me every chance to quit," she says.

At the top he kissed her on the cheek. "Have fun," he said. Then he ran down the hill. He would wait for her at the bottom.

"I was left alone at the top. It was real lonely," she says.

She again saw the pine tree half way down

the hill. But this time she pulled her eyes away from it. She would look at what she wanted to hit, not at what she wanted to avoid.

Three or four minutes went by. Jan did nothing. Finally she went over, bent low, and lifted the glider onto her shoulders. Again she just stood there. She looked like a statue. Then she recalled something Lee told her, "Do not lift the glider until you are ready!" So she put it down.

Another three or four minutes went by. Then all of a sudden she picked up the glider. She snapped on the harness. Down below, Lee cheered. "Looks good! Go for it!" he yelled.

She sure did go for it! She started to run down the hill. But the wind quickly caught her. In 4 steps, she was in the air. "Whoa, I'm flying!" she thought. She was excited. But she was also afraid.

The ride only lasted about 10 seconds. Jan rushed to meet the ground. Just before she hit, she thought, "I don't know how to land."

The bottom of the control bar touched down first. That made the nose dip. Jan tipped over and landed on her head. The impact popped the rivets on her hockey helmet. She sat up. As Lee got to her, she wore a silly grin.

She says, "The whole thing was so quick. Slam! All done! Part of me could not wait to do it again. And part of me never wanted to do it again."

The first part won. She did it again and again. She became a great pilot. Hang gliding became the center of her life. She made gliders. She sold gliders. She taught others how to fly gliders.

In 1975 Jan and Lee split up. They were still friends. But they no longer wanted to be married.

Lee stayed near San Francisco. He could be found most every day on a beach south of San Francisco. There were great hills and wind. It was a perfect spot to hang glide. The other pilots respected Lee. If they had a problem they came to Lee. One day a young pilot came in for a landing. He walked over to Lee. "My glider isn't flying right. Would you try it for me?" he asked.

"Sure. What's it doing?" Lee asked.

"When I speed up, it feels like it wants to turn upside down," he said.

Lee took off with the friend's glider. He flew out over the bright blue Pacific Ocean. The sun was low in the sky. He dipped his wing. Then he eased through a turn. He was now heading back toward the beach.

As he pulled back on the control bar, the glider suddenly ducked. One wing broke. Lee and the glider smashed into the wet sand at the edge of the water.

Jan got a call at the shop. "Lee has gone in," said the voice at the other end. That was a pilot's way of saying that Lee had crashed. Jan rushed to the hospital. She was with him when he died. "I could feel him telling me it was O.K. It wasn't scary. After all, he died doing what he loved to do. And doing it for someone else," she says.

Last year, Jan went back to the spot where Lee died. She stood on the hill with her glider. She was there to fly. But she was also thinking, "Maybe I won't fly. The winds are bad. They are coming from all directions. Maybe I will just sit here."

She was 38 years old now. She was still small and pretty. And she was still in good shape. She could fly in this wind if she wanted. But she was quite content. It was a nice view.

She loved the sport as much as ever. She still had lots of gliders in her garage. And she still flew them several times a year. But maybe today she would not fly. She did not have anything to prove.

She looked out at the Pacific Ocean. She

thought about her friend Eric. Eric had come to Jan for hang-gliding lessons. He was 74 years old. Jan hoped she had inspired Eric. But mostly she thought, "Eric has inspired me. Before I met Eric, I would have launched my glider on a day like today. But Eric is flying at age 74. And when I'm 74, I plan to be flying, too. So even if I don't fly today, I can fly tomorrow. Or the next day. I can fly for the rest of my life. The sport is getting better all the time. So what's the hurry?"

Eric Heiden Beams After a Win

Eric Heiden
Rebel with a Cause

Eric Heiden was on ice skates when he was 2 years old. But he was not happy about it. His father recalls, "Eric fell down a lot. He also whined a lot. 'I'm too little to skate,' he said. I told him, 'O.K., then we will come back next week.' "

They did come back next week. And the week after that. Eric learned to ice skate. Then he learned to ice skate very fast.

But Eric was shown many sports. His whole family was full of athletes. His grandfather had been a hockey player, a swimmer, and a gymnast. His father had been a runner, a fencer, and now was a bicyclist. His mother played a strong game of tennis. She stopped only to have her two children.

Eric's younger sister, Beth, was shown the same sports. She also became a great athlete. Eric says, "We got to try a lot of sports when we were growing up. But our parents never pushed us too hard."

Eric's dad made a large room in their home into a gym. It was there that Eric and Beth had their games of skill. There they had pull-up contests and wrestling matches. Beth says, "For a while we also had a basketball hoop. But the dining room was just a Dutch window away. The ball kept landing on the dinner table. That got old with Mom."

The Heidens' grandparents lived on a lake. Like most Wisconsin lakes, it froze in the winter. Says Eric, "The ice was clear as glass on that lake. It was so clear that we had to skate with a hockey stick ahead of us. We had to make very sure that we did not skate into open water."

Eric and Beth both tried figure skating. But what they really liked was speed skating. They got into "pack racing." That is where all racers start at the same time. It is a mad dash for the finish line. And there is a lot of body contact.

When Eric was 7 and Beth was 5, their uncle entered them in some city races. Says Eric, "I remember standing at the starting line shaking in my skates. But I won my race. I think Beth did, too. After that we were both recruited by the local speed skating club."

Eric grew up solid and strong. He had huge thighs. Those are important muscles in skating. He was strong enough to take care of himself in a crowd of skaters. But he still changed from pack racing to "metric skating." Only two skaters are on the ice at the same time in metric skating. That is the way they skate in the Olympics. So that is the way he would do it.

When Eric was 16, he made the Junior

World Team. He got to go to Europe and race. Europe was great, but he did not race well. He fell in the Junior World Championships and finished 10th. Yet he still felt good about the future. "I felt like I was over the hump. I now knew that if I worked hard, I could make the Olympics," he says.

He had the talent. He had the winning outlook. Now all he needed was a coach. Then Diane Holum came to town. She had won an Olympic gold medal in speed skating. And she wanted to be a coach. Eric says, "She was great. In the next 6 or 7 years, 15 local skaters made the world team. It was all because of her."

Diane made her skaters work hard. Eric trained twice a day, 5 days a week. He skated a lot. But he also ran, lifted weights, and bicycled. Eric has always loved to work out. Most people do not feel that way. He says, "My secret is that I like it. I like setting goals. I also like reaching goals. That is what makes me happy. I get a good feeling reaching a goal that I set."

Says Diane, "Eric was about 14 when he started training real hard. He was in with a lot of other kids who also trained hard. Most of them leveled off after one year. They stopped getting better. Eric did, too. A lot of the other kids quit. But Eric didn't quit. He just kept on. Sometimes I wonder why."

Maybe Eric could see what the future held for him. In 1976 he made the Olympic team. He says, "The 1976 Olympics was in Austria. I had a blast." He sounds like a little kid talking about his first trip to Disney World. He adds, "The Olympic Village was our own little town. There was good food, free pin ball, good tunes. The problem was, I was not thinking about racing. And I sure was not thinking about winning. I was too happy to be there. My goal had been to make the Olympic team. I forgot there was more to be done."

When he went back to high school in Madison, a girl he knew said to him, "Wow, the Olympics. How are you going to top that?"

"You wait," he said. "I'm going to be world champion."

Eric remembered something his dad told him. "If you want to be a champion, you have to train like a champion," he liked to say. Eric was at last ready to listen to his dad's advice.

Diane increased Eric's workouts. Now he worked out twice a day, 6 days a week. Then he often did a single workout on the 7th day. He says, "There is another reason I like to work out. It is great how it feels when I'm done. I work out for a couple of hours, then sit down with a big plate of food. And I feel so good about it. I feel like I earned it." Eric laughs. "One time after a workout, three of us bought a whole cake and ate it."

Eric's hard work paid off. When he was 18,

he won the Speed Skating World Championship. To do that meant he had to be the best overall skater after 4 races. First he won the shortest one, the 500 meter race. Then he finished 3rd in the 1,500 meters. After that, he finished 9th in the 5,000. That was the way it often went for Americans. The longer the race, the worse they did. No one gave Eric much chance in the last race. It was 10,000 meters long. That is about 6 miles of hard skating.

His best time ever in the 10,000 was 15 minutes, 27 seconds. He needed a 15:02 to be all-around champ. It did not seem possible.

Eric was paired with Olympic champ Piet Kleine. It would be just the two of them skating around the oval track at the same time. But Eric was really racing against the clock.

For the first five miles, they were dead even. Eric matched Piet stroke for stroke, skate for skate. They changed lanes every lap. That kept the length of the race the same for both men. Eric's father thought the two skaters looked very graceful. "Like two geese in flight," he called the racers.

At the end, Eric reached back for an extra burst. He put on a strong sprint and finished in 14:59. It was 28 seconds faster than his best time! He was the World Speed Skating Champ. He was also the first American since 1891 who could say that.

Eric's win pushed him to work even harder. He had to prove the best man had won. He had to prove his win was no mistake. He could do that by winning an Olympic gold medal.

In the 3 years before the 1980 Olympics, Eric lost only 2 races. One of those losses bothers him more than any defeat in his life. It also says a lot about what kind of guy Eric is. He says, "It happened at the 1978 World Championships in Sweden. Back then the rules were different. There were 4 races. If you won the first 3 races, you were champ, no matter where you finished in the fourth race. You just had to finish. So I won the first 3 races. And then I finished eighth in the last race. I felt bad. I had never blown a race that way. And I had never given up like that. I was World Champion, but I was upset with myself. It taught me something. You cannot try to please other people. You have to please yourself."

He pleased himself a lot in the 1980 Olympics. The games were at Lake Placid, New York. He says, "It was great having the Olympics in the United States. This time I thought about nothing else but racing. But it was hard racing every other day. I never really had a day off. I was either racing or getting ready for the next race. And I did not sleep much."

Who needs much sleep? Not Eric. In between naps, he raced his heart out. He entered 5 races. When it was over, he had five gold medals, five Olympic records and one world record. Nobody had ever won that many gold medals at a Winter Olympics.

Eric was picked in Europe as Best Male Athlete of 1980. But in the United States, they gave the honor to the U.S. hockey team. Some people thought Eric would be mad. They did not know him very well. He was happy that the hockey team won the gold medal. And he was happy that it took attention away from him. He told the New York Times, "I like people not knowing who I am. If they know who I am, they come and ask me to pose for pictures. And they ask the same questions over and over. It gets kind of boring—except that sometimes I get to meet some nice girls."

That is how he talks. He's just like one of the guys. He won 5 Olympic gold medals, but now he can't even find them. He says, "I am not impressed with gold medals. I am impressed by people who work hard. If you win but don't work hard, so what?"